What a wonderful (everyone has experier has taken these mome Christ to help us remei .... laughter and love in our life. I highly recommend keeping *Life is a Yo-Yo* handy for those moments when a "picker-upper" is needed in your day—it will bring a smile to your face and warm your heart.

Cathy Hersom, Children's Ministries Director
Church of the Servant

Wild and witty, Merry Weatherbee will delight your girlfriends and feel like an afternoon chatting with a good friend. Sisters of all ages will be blessed.

Jane Pickelsimer, RN

Penny Stephenson is an inspirational speaker who motivates her listeners with her humor and wit. With her book, *Life is a Yo-Yo*, she will have you laughing, crying and contemplating all within a matter of minutes.

Lynda K. Powell, Founder of Bethel Foundation

Merry's wit and wisdom is infectious. I've truly enjoyed sharing this little novelty of life with friends and colleagues and hope the owner of this book will make it accessible for others to read. I think you will find it the perfect compliment for a coffee table or night stand.

Gary Owen, Professional Comedian

A true inspiration. Witty and funny! It gets to the fabric of life.

Ella Sprung, Membership Director
Edmond Area Chamber of Commerce

What would life be like without the Lord's gift of laughter?
Penny's rhymes show us the humorous side of everyday life, a delightful blessing that helps us to take ourselves a little less seriously.

Gayla White, Director
Hope Pregnancy Center North

Penny has a joyful outlook on life and a special gift for communicating her faith. In this book, she offers women of all ages and stages encouragement through her lighthearted and uplifting prose.

Patti Benton, Ph.D

God has gifted Penny with the ability to take the mundane and make it marvelous, with her keen wit, wisdom, and inspiration. A quick read for those moments when life seems too overwhelming. The common threads that run through the book, will give you a connectedness that will make you smile and laugh out loud, as you appreciate Merry Weatherbee's perspective on the simpler things of life.

Suzy Wolfe, Accounting Mgr/HR

Life is a Yo-Yo

Life is a Yo-Yo

Merry Weatherbee

TATE PUBLISHING & *Enterprises*

Life is a Yo-Yo
Copyright © 2009 by Penny Stephenson. All rights reserved.

No part of this publication may be reproduced, stored in a retrieval system or transmitted in any way by any means, electronic, mechanical, photocopy, recording or otherwise without the prior permission of the author except as provided by USA copyright law.

The opinions expressed by the author are not necessarily those of Tate Publishing, LLC.

Published by Tate Publishing & Enterprises, LLC
127 E. Trade Center Terrace | Mustang, Oklahoma 73064 USA
1.888.361.9473 | www.tatepublishing.com

Tate Publishing is committed to excellence in the publishing industry. The company reflects the philosophy established by the founders, based on Psalm 68:11,
"The Lord gave the word and great was the company of those who published it."

Book design copyright © 2009 by Tate Publishing, LLC. All rights reserved.
Cover design by Kandi Evans
Interior design by Joey Garrett
Illustrated by Debbie Weekly

Published in the United States of America

ISBN: 978-1-60799-461-9
Poetry / Inspirational
09.08.18

Dedication

To my loving husband, Craig, and wonderful children, Travis and Lauren, who fill my life with love, laughter, and zesty spice!—And who inspire many observations.

Observing life in the rhyme of schemes...

Table of Contents

Foreword

It is a delightful thing to meet Penny. You are immediately taken by her beautiful smile and infectious laugh, which is bound to surface within seconds after meeting her. She is a happy and positive person, totally in love with God and with people. Shortly after I met Penny, she invited me into her home, where I found what I refer to as the "Merry Room." It is full of color, outrageously wonderful hats and accessories, and creative memorabilia. I noticed the open Bible on her kitchen table, where she was working on a current Bible study. Her daily walk with God seemed to be reflected in her home as well as in her conversations. She gave me a couple of her "Merry" books, and I took them with me to read. I quickly realized that I wanted to introduce all of my friends to Merry and her wonderful view on life. My church invited her to our women's retreat, and from her very entrance, she gave us all I could have dreamed of and more.

Penny calls Merry "a life observer," but as she bounces into your women's event, showering "howdy's" and smiles on everyone, you soon realize she is much more than that. Although it is true that she dispenses the retelling of life's situations with wit, humor, and grace, she delves further into them. She explores situations and relationships with God's wisdom, and draws us into thoughtful and challenging conclusions. You hardly realize at first how your heart is being touched, because you are having such fun and laughing so hard.

I heartily recommend Merry Weatherbee to you. Read with enjoyment, but be prepared—you may never be the same!

—Davidene Humphreys
National Speaker/Author
Oklahoma City

Life is a Yo-Yo

Life is a Yo-Yo
Full of ups and downs,
One minute you're home free,
The next … out of bounds.

It's part of the mystery
That's ever unfoldin',
Like how penicillin
Is made from cheese moldin'.

But one thing's for sure
When life gets you down,
God works toward your good,
So quit wearin' that frown.

Oh, it's easier to say
Than to live by this promise,
But he made a believer
Out of "Doubting Thomas!"

He'll turn negatives to positives
With his powerful pardon.
Make our old life of rubbish
Rich compost for his garden!

He'll turn pain into gain,
He'll make bitter, all better!
Turn tragedy to triumph,
And free every debtor!

Why, remember Simple Simon?
And that ol' Persecutor Saul?
Christ transformed those men
To Saints Peter and Paul!

Yes, change is the secret,
And it's not always fast.
But give God your troubles,
And he'll build things that last!

This great God of old,
Is our same God for today.
But the secret to seeing,
Is to trust and obey.

Mercy and goodness
Shall follow your days,
Mercy and goodness,
So give God your praise!

Oh, life is a yo-yo,
And I've been bounced all around,
But Christ never forsakes me,
And lifts me up, when I'm down!

Knick Knacks

Knick knacks are small,
About 12 inches or under.
Some are real art pieces,
While some make you wonder!

But the beauty is in the eye
Of the knick knack beholder.
What may look like a soup can
May be someone's candle holder!

From cut glass to crystal,
Wooden carvin's to clay pots,
Every shape, size, and material,
From gold monkeys to pet rocks!

Knick knacks are important;
They give homes an expression.
They bring warmth to cold spaces
And leave a lasting impression.

Now most husbands complain,
In ridiculous mutter,
That "Knick knacks are nothin'
But pure household clutter!"

"They're senseless, they're petty,
They're nothin' but junk!
Everywhere I turn
There's frivolous funk!"

"There's no room for me
To shell my peanuts!
No place for my drink can
Or to practice my putts!"

"There's a basket of apples,
There's a duck and a vase—
There're too many knick knacks
Invading my space!"

Well… he may have a point,
I'll have to admit.
But knock out my knick knacks?
I must think and outwit.

I'll run out tomorrow
For a peanut bowl and tray
Some cute, trendy coasters
And a golf game to play.

What a nice compromise
To shop for his snacks!
But Shhhh, just don't tell him,
They're really—knick knacks!

A Sack of Potatoes

Have you ever noticed
Any food store you're in,
When it comes to potatoes,
There's just no way to win?

Be it five pounds or ten,
Any sack that you choose,
Whatever the price—
You're just bound to lose.

'Cause in every sack
Of spuds that I've gotten,
There's always one tater
That always is rotten!

And it spreads its disease-
In its close range of path,
Until three or four more,
Are destroyed by its wrath!

It remind me of life,
In the most general of terms—
Where ever you go,
There're always those worms,

Who infest honest work,
With the dirtiest of deeds—
Be it plumber or banker,
Or a kennel that breeds!

It's a dog-eat-dog world,
It's a world full of crime,
But it's all just a matter of
How you spend your time.

Oh it's tons more easy
Just to look the other way,
But give into pressure,
And you'll be French fried someday!

So take heed from those spuds,
That got too close by mistake—
Stay way from potato-heads,
Who go around.... half baked!

The "Honey Do" List

Those sweet little chores
That men can't refuse,
Are affectionately called,
The "Honey Do's!"

Tho' try as they might
To put off and delay,
These chores must be done,
By sunset, Sunday!

Now, the "Honey Do" list
Requires much finesse,
It takes delicate wording,
Plus a soft, warm caress.

And the woman who's smart
Might sweeten the pot
By cooking the meal
That her man likes a lot.

Be it fixing the washer,
Or the sink with a leak,
These lists are accrued
All through the week.

Sometimes you must barter
And trade for his time,
A weekend of duty
For a weekend sublime.

Like golfing or fishing,
Camping out with the guys—
It's the perfect incentive
For the woman who's wise.

Oh, I know it seems silly,
All the games we must play,
To motivate men
On their Honey-Do Day.

But you've got to admit,
Even men will agree—
The sweeter the nectar,
The busier the bee!

So from paintin' the fence
To ceilings above,
Make your "Honey Do" list,
A labor of love!

Sale-A-Holic

I am a Sale-a-Holic,
I humbly confess.
I'll set out to buy shoes
And come back with a dress!

It's purely unplanned,
Though try as I might,
I can't pass up a store
With a "SALE" sign in sight!

I'll tell myself over
And over again,
Its shoes that I want—
Not another red hen!

My heels are worn out,
There're holes in my soles.
I need something to cover
My bare little toes!

Then off to the mall,
Fortified with will power!
I promise myself to be gone—
Just one hour.

As I open the door,
I slowly inhale …
To my morbid elation,
There's a sidewalk sale!

My mind starts to whirl
Like leaves in late autumn,
At five acres of merchandise
Slashed down to rock bottom!

There're clothes for my kids,
Knit shirts for my hubby,
Some cute candlesticks
That'll look nice in my cubby.

Look at these savings;
Over fifty percent!
These earrings will add
Just the perfect accent!

Ten bucks for this skirt?
Oh, I must try it on.
That pattern is lovely,
A purple octagon!

I shop and I save
'Til I'm down to one cent.
I look at my watch
And four hours I have spent!

So I go home half happy,
Half singin' the blues.
I saved lots of money,
But I can't afford shoes!

Hide 'n Seek

Hide and Seek is a game
That we learn from our youth.
It demands that our playmate
Must seek out the truth.

Now as we grow older,
This game still applies,
As we play with our spouse
In order not to tell lies.

Though the game is quite subtle,
Even the hider's unaware,
That he's tucked something away
To avoid a mad glare.

It occurs in both sexes,
When a budget is tight,
Someone buys something
That might cause a big fight!

Like a rod for his fishin,'
A dress for her party,
Golf clubs or car mats,
Bric-a-brac that is "arty."

And instead of enjoyin'
Our prize with our spouse,
We secretly stash it
Somewhere in the house.

Under beds, on high shelves,
In the cupboard or car trunk.
Then we revel in silence
Like a reclusive old monk.

We wait and we scheme,
'Til the time is just right,
To unveil our treasure
In our spouse's plain sight.

Well… that's usually the plan,
Though it never wins out,
'Cause somehow our seeker,
They always find out!

And no matter how clever
You tried to conceal it,
By some quirk of events
Your spouse will reveal it!

Then you're busted of course
And there's explainin' to do.
A confession perhaps,
And apology too?

So learn from the game
That you played in your youth.
Whatever you hide,
You can't hide from the truth!

Weekend Widow

I grieve for the wife
Whose husband loves sports,
'Cause when weekends roll by—
He's like a dead corpse!

Though his body is present
And functions quite well,
His mind's in a trance,
Under some kind of spell …

Watching football or hockey,
Or a golf tournament.
There's baseball, of course,
Which brings much lament,

For the wife of this man
'Cause there're hundreds of games,
Before one team, finally,
The World Series claims!

Now, some games are so big,
They require a watch party—
With beer, pretzels, and bean dip,
And a loudmouth named Marty!

Both stereo and TV
Are cranked up to the max.
There's hootin' and hollerin'
'Til your ears are quite taxed!

Then once the show's over,
The winners, overjoyed,
They leave one by one
From your house they destroyed!

Now there are also those men
Who jump into the game
And leave every weekend
To claim their own fame!

Either hunting or fishing
Or golf is quite par,
For our men to obsess on
It's really bizarre!

And these poor weekend widows
Are stuck home with the kids,
While their husbands go play,
Or make bets on their bids.

But try as men might
To be athletes of sorts,
It's their wives left behind
Who're really the best sports!

The Housewife Dilemma

The pendulum of life
Is a curious thing…
One day you're on course,
The next, out of swing.

Take housewives, for instance,
The professional kind—
Yesterday there were many
Today, hard to find.

The reasons for this
Are all very valid,
Staying home for some women,
Makes 'em feel like fruit salad!

Especially when children
Are under age four,
Taking care of these tots
Is a tremendous chore!

Changing the diapers
And the beds that they wet,
Cleaning hundreds of spills—
On that, you can bet!

You pick up, they mess up,
It's a daily routine.
Thank goodness for Clorox
And 'ol Mr. Clean!

Dust, mop, and vacuum,
Fix three meals a day.
Wash, iron, and watch kids
Without one cent of pay!

Oh, paying 'em, oh,
Well, that's never the story.
It must be because
Housewives get all that glory!

And to top it all off
The world questions her choice
To be a stay-at-home mother
And ridicules her voice.

And that's just not fair
For the lady of the house,
Not only does she work free,
But made to feel like a louse!

How many of us often
Take housewives for granted?
No pats on the back
Or much praise ever chanted.

Economics is one thing,
And careers are another,
But some women just want to be
The best wife and best mother!

That's a commendable thing
And it should be encouraged.
Not belittled or patronized
'Cause it takes lots of courage!

So hail to the housewife
As she shines up the chrome!
Be it ever so humble,
Her office is her home!

Children at Best

I like children best
When they are asleep.
They're angelic and charming
And don't make a peep.

Oh, now don't get me wrong,
I love them awake,
But it's amazing to me
All the things they can break!

I once had a jar
That was made in Japan,
And now, it's exported
To the kitchen trash can.

My crystal candy dish?
The question never ceases
At just how it could shatter
Into so many small pieces!

From pottery to china
If you want my advice,
I think all things
Should be made like "Fisher-Price!"

And speakin' of which,
It's mind bogglin' to me
That the millions we spend
On toys, don't you see—

Are never as much fun
As the things in high places,
Like my plates and tea cups
And my Indian vases.

Now as children grow older,
The breakage is less extensive,
But the things that teens break
Are much more expensive!

Like the car—the lawn mower,
Or our washing machines!
Over loading the laundry
With twelve pair of blue jeans!

But kids have their moments,
And they make me feel blessed,
Especially when—
They lay down for a rest!

Couch Collectibles

I was cleaning one day,
As I've done lots before—
But my mother was coming,
So I cleaned down to the core!

I was vacuuming cobwebs
In ceilings above.
Working hard and preparing
For that "little white glove."

And the stuff that I cleaned,
Made me feel like a slouch.
Especially when
I look inside my couch!

It was like a lost treasure
Of things that were missing,
Some things were so old,
I enjoyed reminiscing.

There were old G. I. Joes,
One missing blue sock,
A few hair pins and coins,
A red comb and padlock.

Some peanuts leftover
From the last football game,
And a snap shot I'd lost,
That I wanted to frame.

As I flipped up the cushions
Discovering these things,
I delightfully found,
My favorite earrings!

It was like this old couch
That we sit on each day,
Secretly picked pockets
Then hid things away.

Now I know it sounds silly
To think couches may eat—
But they do have a back,
Some arms, legs, and seat.

So couldn't it be
That a couch has a tummy?
To munch on those treats
It considers quite yummy?

How long has it been
Since you took a peek,
Under your cushions,
Six months, or a week?

Well, the longer you wait
And the more you're neglectible,
The chances are great
To find a couch collectible!

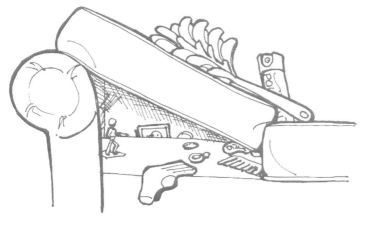

Driving with Your Spouse

Whate're your destination,
Or distance near or far,
There's a strange transformation
To couples in a car.

The change is in both sexes,
It is a two-way street—
But it usually happens to the one
Who's in the driver's seat!

In my case it's my husband
Who gets behind the wheel.
No sooner does he turn the key,
His baby blues turn cold steel.

His gentle loving ways take flight,
Replaced with rage and furry.
He's like "Rambo" in a tank
And always in a hurry!

The roads become a jungle,
With insufficient signs
To tell him where he's going,
Or proper exit lines.

But to stop and ask directions
To steer us back on course,
Is "Silly, dumb, ridiculous!"
(It leads to near divorce.)

The other drivers on the road,
In front and back and flanks,
Are "bozos, jerks, and pin-heads,"
And other blankety-blanks!

I challenged him one time
And said to Mr. Weatherbee,
"For the next five minutes
I request a little courtesy!"

"No more words of venom,
Like an angry hornets hive.
Be pleasant or be silent,
But let's enjoy the drive!"

Well, he nodded in agreement,
With a little demon's smile—
He turned the tables on me,
But he did it with great style.

"Wasn't that nice," he said to me,
"Of that driver to cut in front,
The guy behind me eatin' bumpers,
Now that's a tricky stunt!"

"These detour signs are lovely,
Right on the interstate,
Which makes us take the scenic route,
So now we're really late!"

Well, this went on for miles and miles,
With acid tongue and cheek.
He changed his tone but not his tune
With masterful technique!

"All right, all ready!" I blurted out,
You've made your point quite clear,
You're the best driver on the road!"
(My sneer was insincere.)

He winked and made me laugh
As he drove back to the house.
But sometimes it drives me crazy,
When driving with my spouse!

Friendships

A friend is a person
You let into your heart.
Be it man or a woman
You can tell them apart,

From the rest of the crowd
That may always surround you,
'Cause a friend is the one
Who will never confound you

With a lot of silly gossip
Or political games.
You don't have to impress 'em
By dropping big names.

'Cause when it comes down to friendships,
Really, none of that matters.
Nor the way you may dress,
Or if your blue jeans have tatters.

I guess with close friends
There's a definite chemistry—
An unspoken bond
That is ever a mystery.

But, just as in all things,
A bond can be broken.
So don't treat your friendships
Like a haphazard token.

It's a nurturing process
That you build as you grow,
Closer together through life's
Ebb and flow.

Trust, love, and respect
Are the most basic of needs
For a friendship to manifest
Its wonderful deeds!

The laughs that are shared,
The tears that are shed,
The comfort of knowing
If you go head-to-head—

Your friendship will endure
All the things that were said,
As long as you forgive
And not hold grudges, instead.

Oh, a rich one are you,
Who claims just one at his side,
That when trouble draws near
They won't run and hide,

But will be ever faithful
To their friend who's in need.
Then that my dear friends
Is a real friend in deed!

Grocery Shopping

If more politicians
Would grocery shop each week,
The problem of budget balancing,
Would become obsolete.

Now this is a challenge
That requires fortitude,
Turnin' X amount of dollars
Into a week's worth of food.

But this task is not easy,
More like forging up hills,
Pushing wobbly carts
Through narrow aisles full of spills!

It's bumper to bumper—
Children running in between—
Someone's caused a big jam
And you just want to scream!

Then just when you think
The line will never move on,
The one causin' this mess
Yells, "I found my coupon!"

So two hours later,
Much time as been lost,
Comparin' prices and labels
'Til your eyes are quite crossed.

It's time to check out
And check off your list,
Only to discover a few things
That you missed!

While the checker is checking
You run fast as you can,
Grab some mayo and mustard,
And improved roll on Ban.

The total is tallied,
And you're three dollars short!
But it's double coupon day,
So you frantically sort

Through your clippings and stamps
And you pray as you go,
"Please help me find fifty cents off
Miracle Grow!"

Now all coupons are added,
And subtracted this time.
The new total finds
That you get back a dime!

A sigh is expelled!
And your color restored!
The budget is balanced,
Thanks to the Good Lord!

So statesmen, take note!
And learn from your spouse,
That all things are possible—
Even budgeting the White House!

House Plants

I pity the plant
That comes into my house,
'Cause its days are soon numbered,
Like a laboratory mouse.

I know it seems cruel,
But I'm not really mean...
I'm just one of those ladies
Whose thumb won't turn green!

My petunias look puny.
My poppies poop out.
My cactus just croaks.
And my seedlings won't sprout!

But I water and feed 'em,
Allow plenty of sun.
Some plants are particular—
I keep forgetting which one.

I sometimes play music,
The elevator kind,
I was told plants enjoy this
And grow quite refined.

But Sinatra and Streisand
Must sing through much static,
'Cause my radio is old;
It came down from the attic.

And instead of new growth
And graceful long stems,
My plants all look fried,
Full of short, broken limbs!

And try as I might
To sustain just one flower,
They all wither and die.
It's just not in my power!

So I'll give up the soil
And won't cry over spilt milk.
From now on my houseplants,
Will be all made of—silk!

People, people
who need.....

Living Color

Roses are red
And violets are blue,
But there's a lot more to colors
From an emotional sense of hue.

Take for instance those things
That we term Black and White,
It refers to those virtues
Of what's wrong and what's right.

Gray is an area
Where emotions are mixed;
There're no quick decisions
Or problems easily fixed.

You're either hot or you're cold
Or you're warm or you're cool.
But color degrees are what
Best describe this rule.

If you're Hot Pink, you're sassy.
Red Hot, full of spice.
But Steel Blue is the opposite,
Meanin' you're just cold as ice.

The colors we choose
To describe our emotions
Are much more on target
Than fancy words by the oceans!

You're either Green with envy,
Or singin' the Blues—
Which means that you're jealous,
Or just filled with sad news.

Red can mean anger,
And Purple, full of passion,
But when you wear them together
Then you're highly in fashion!

When life is good and healthy,
Then you're feeling "In the Pink"
But a business is bummed out
When there's too much Red Ink.

A Black Sheep in the family
Will pull the wool over your eyes,
Like a Silver-Tongued Devil
Who tells silky smooth lies.

If you're Yellow—you're chicken
Or so I've been told,
But when cowards turn heroes,
They're as Good as Gold!

So, if you're White as a ghost
Or a loyal True Blue,
There's a colorful sayin',
That I'm sure will fit you!

GOLD

Mother's Day Out

Every once in a while
My husband will say,
"It's your turn to go out.
Have your own holiday."

"I'll watch the kids,
And fix dinner tonight,
So have a good time
We'll be all right!"

Once I pick up my jaw,
Which falls shocked on the floor,
I grab for my purse
And run out the door!

What a happy surprise,
To be treated this way.
A "Mother's Day Out"
When it's not Mother's Day!

So I'll check out that sale
At that cute dress boutique,
Then I'll browse a short while
For a brand new antique.

The book store and gift shop
Are places to hit.
Then it's time for a bite,
And a short chance to sit.

My how times flies
When you're having such fun,
So I turn to head home
Towards the setting sun.

As I roll in the driveway
There are bicycles scattered,
With a couple of T-shirts
Tossed off and left tattered.

I walk into the house
Which is now a pigpen!
There are toys by the zillions
All over the den!

The beds are unmade,
There's still food out from lunch.
Dinner is McDonald's,
I have a strong hunch!

And there's Dad and the kids,
All watching TV,
Munching burnt popcorn
And as happy as can be!

Well, that is the main thing,
So I really can't pout.
But we pay heavily
For our "Mother's Day Out!"

The Family Dinner

It's scary sometimes
When you ponder the day,
At just how many moments
Are shared along the way.

From the moment we wake,
The family's dispersed,
Like a never-ending play,
Yet, totally unrehearsed.

Dad gets his morning shower
While the kids are getting dressed.
You grab a cup of coffee
And make sure they brush with Crest.

Then filing in for breakfast
Never happens as a unit;
No time for eggs and bacon,
You just pour it out and spoon it.

One sits down, the other gets up
And 'round and 'round they go.
And one by one, a kiss goodbye
To work or school—you know.

When school lets out, all heck breaks loose,
There's dance class and cub scouts.
Band and football practice, too,
And cheerleader tryouts!

Your husband's home by six o'clock;
The day is finally done—
But dinner time is eat and run,
For the night time has begun!

There's P.T.A. and play practice,
Or church or business meetings.
By the time you all convene again,
There's a sleepy exchange of greetings.

So another day has zoomed right by
Filled with monosyllables:
"Yes" or "No" and "Fine" or "Sure,"
With no blanks fill-able.

Used to, it was dinner time,
When all would feast and talk,
About the day's activities
And other food for thought.

But even with our microwaves
That make meals in seconds flat—
It seems our lives are much too rushed
For a sit-down dinner chat.

One hour a day to sit and talk,
Is that so much to ask?
To convene as one whole body,
From the first-born to the last?

Yes, be it beanie-weenies,
Or a rib of beef that's prime,
There's no food finer for the soul
Than chewin' the fat at dinner time!

BEANIE·WEENIES

"Waiting In Line"

There's no greater irritation,
At least, that is mine,
Than the time we must waste,
Just waiting in line!

There's no way to escape it,
No lessons to learn,
Wherever we go
We must all wait our turn.

The grocery or drug store,
The post office, too.
A movie or dinner,
The bank or the zoo.

Of course rush hour traffic
Brings on much stress,
Especially when
The roads are a mess!

With construction and detours,
Plus, a one-lane bottle-neck.
By the time I get home,
I'm the one who's a wreck!

Now most of these things
Are out of our hands.
There's no way to avoid 'em
Under the best laid plans.

But the ones who astound me,
Are the folks who don't mind,
Waiting hours, maybe days
To see a rock star wail and grind!

What force can it be?
That drives people to exert
So much of their lives
For a two-hour concert!

It makes as much sense
As the hours we bide
In a roller coaster line
For a two-minute ride!

Oh, it all seems so foolish
To just stand there in rows,
Sweatin' or freezin',
Rubbin' corns on your toes.

The big question, I guess,
To be able to measure
The fun that you had, is—
"Was the wait worth the pleasure?"

If the answer is, "Yes,"
Then you'll think it's just fine,
To quickly run back,
And start waiting in line!

Weeds

A weed is a plant
That we don't plant at all.
They'll grow in your garden,
Your yard—on a wall!

And year after year,
We pluck and we pull
Thousands of weeds,
About ten trash bags full.

Now this is a mystery,
To me, that's amazing!
How a weed can come back
After abusive, hard hazing!

All the money we spend
On grass, plants, and seeds,
But the only survivors
Are always the weeds!

Through the harshest of winters
And poisons we spread,
The Dandelion blooms first
In our spring flower bed!

Johnson and Crab grass
Are the first to be seen,
Before Tiff and Bermuda
Start to make our yards green.

Through floods and hard droughts;
The weeds persevere.
For the rose and holly bush,
The weather was too severe.

To endure all those hardships,
And never say "Quit,"
To live on the edge,
Hanging on by true grit!

To bloom faithful in seasons
In the midst of rejection,
It reminds me of Jesus,
Right before His Resurrection!

Yes, God plants His seeds
Of wisdom and knowledge,
In all of creation.
It's His glorified college!

It's not strength or great beauty
That weeds have to boast,
Rather patience and endurance
Are the things I learn most.

And this, I suppose,
Is what makes me concede
And desire to grow more
Like that little old weed!

Look on the Bright Side

When life deals out lemons
Don't be too dismayed.
Just add sugar and water
And make lemonade!

Oh, it's not always easy
To find the bright side,
Most times we'd much rather
Go run off and hide!

But no matter the problems
That you face for today,
God will work it all out,
If you'll trust and obey.

If it weren't for the pot holes
In the highways of life,
If it weren't for the setbacks,
The detours and strife—

What would prompt us to change?
And to care and to grow?
There's always a rainfall
Right before the rainbow.

My dear 'Nana' used to say,
"Things happen for the best."
And for 93 years,
These words she practiced.

Throughout The Great Depression
With six children to raise,
She and her husband
Gave thanks and gave praise!

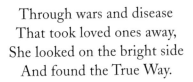

Through wars and disease
That took loved ones away,
She looked on the bright side
And found the True Way.

There are those who see nothing
But negatives first.
They almost enjoy
Discovering the worst,

In their friends and their jobs
And mostly their life—
Always cutting things down
With a pessimistic knife.

Perhaps they are blind
Or very near-sighted,
To all of their blessings
That God has provided.

An ungrateful heart
Is never content,
'Cause its focus is on
What is always absent.

Is the cup half empty?
Or half full in your eyes?
Is the problem a burden?
Or a blessing in disguise?

It depends on your view
From your faith, deep inside.
But the view is much brighter
When Christ's light is your guide!

This is Merry Weatherbee, observing life
in the rhyme of schemes.
--bye, bye now

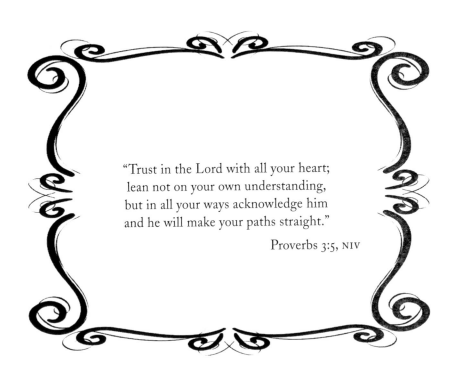

"Trust in the Lord with all your heart;
lean not on your own understanding,
but in all your ways acknowledge him
and he will make your paths straight."

Proverbs 3:5, NIV